Run Benny Run!

Kathy Bingham Powell

AuthorHouse™
1663 Liberty Drive
Bloomington, IN 47403
www.authorhouse.com
Phone: 833-262-8899

Because of the dynamic nature of the Internet, any web addresses or links contained in this book may have changed since publication and may no longer be valid. The views expressed in this work are solely those of the author and do not necessarily reflect the views of the publisher, and the publisher hereby disclaims any responsibility for them.

Any people depicted in stock imagery provided by Getty Images are models, and such images are being used for illustrative purposes only.
Certain stock imagery © Getty Images.

This book is printed on acid-free paper.

ISBN: 978-1-4634-2851-8 (sc)

Library of Congress Control Number: 2011910903

Print information available on the last page.

Published by AuthorHouse 10/13/2021

authorHOUSE®

I would like to dedicate this book to my loving husband and three children for all their encouragement and support and to all my Kinder Gardeners who share with me the joy of planting seeds and growing God's fruit.

It was a beautiful spring day and the promise of warm weather filled the air.

Flowers were beginning to bloom in the back of the garden. Iris, who was always an early riser, was already up and dressed in her beautiful Easter attire. She had been reunited with her former friends, Dolly the daffodil and Teresa the tulip. With the celebration of spring, everyone knew it was time to plant the summer garden.

Once again, the tiny seeds felt themselves being planted into the cool, damp, freshly tilled soil of the little vegetable garden.

As Benny, the tiny "half-runner" string bean seed, was planted into the small hole, he dreamed! Because he had been saved, he would grow into another beautiful plant in the garden again that summer.

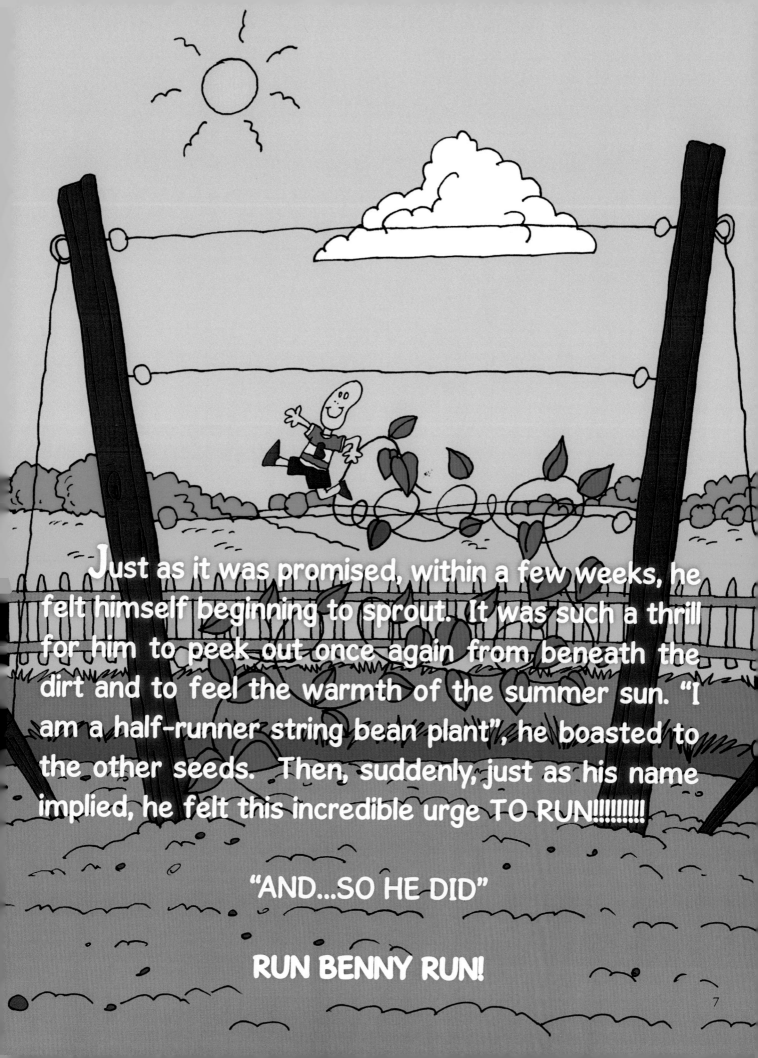

Just as it was promised, within a few weeks, he felt himself beginning to sprout. It was such a thrill for him to peek out once again from beneath the dirt and to feel the warmth of the summer sun. "I am a half-runner string bean plant", he boasted to the other seeds. Then, suddenly, just as his name implied, he felt this incredible urge TO RUN!!!!!!!!!!

"AND...SO HE DID"

RUN BENNY RUN!

It seemed as though he grew an inch every day straight up to the sky. Soon, Benny found himself getting so tall that he could hardly stand up anymore. He gleefully dove toward the dirt again once more. "This is great," he thought to himself. "I love the dirt! Only now I will not have to stay planted in one place anymore. I am free to explore all around the little vegetable garden." There was so much to see and so little time for him to see it all..........but his plans soon changed.

Soon after Benny's travel began, he felt the warm and gentle touch of the gardener's hands. His running plans were interrupted as he felt himself being lifted up carefully from the dirt floor of the garden. Ever so gently he was guided around a tiny string, which was tied to two strong stakes in the ground. To his surprise, suddenly he was able to see a beautiful blue sky and felt once again the warmth of THE SUN.

Benny was happy with his higher position, for a while, but missed the former freedom of roaming around the garden. He was able to see the sky and feel the presence of the sun, but he still reminded himself that he was a special bean seed and that he was "born to run". The dreams of exploring the garden and his strong desire to make his own choices about where and how he grew seem to overwhelm his thoughts.

He cried out, "I want to express my own free will to do the things I want to do!!"

Every day he continued to feel the gardener's gentle hands try to guide his growth up towards THE SUN, but everyday he became more and more determined to have it his way and began to stubbornly refuse to wind around the tiny strings. It became easier and easier for him to slip away from the touch of the gardener as he became bigger and stronger. Each day, the hands would gently guide him around the strings and each night he would unwind and try to find his own way.

Then one day after a heavy rain Benny found himself able to totally slip away from the wet strings and fall free to the ground. To his surprise and excitement, he was once again on the dirt floor of the garden. The soil, which was damp from the rains, reassured him that the gardener would not be back for a couple of days. This was his chance to fulfill his dreams and exercise his free will – NO strings attached!

Benny began to roam the garden and make his own decisions. There were no guidelines anymore and he was free to grow where, when, and how he wanted to grow. Without thinking about anything or anybody but himself, Benny, the half-runner, was running as fast as he could. Free will was a wonderful thing........

OR AT LEAST HE THOUGHT IT WAS!

It wasn't too long before Benny had climbed all over his pea buddies and trespassed onto the property of his cucumber pals. AND, he became so full of himself and his free will that he soon found himself in one giant twisted mess with his "mater" neighbors.

Being so wrapped up in making his own choices, he never once even considered that as he was moving away from the sun, he was also moving away from what he was meant to do and hurting the growth of the other vegetables. Benny found himself all alone with no blooms to call his own. In this twisted mess he would not grow anymore and would never be able to produce any green beans.

From the back of the garden, he heard his friend, Iris, call to him, "B-E-N-N-Y! What are you thinking? Don't you remember why you are special and for whom you were saved?"

In the meantime, he also heard the complaints of those around him.

"What's the matter with you?" shouted Zelda, the zipper crème pea.

"That's my dirt!!" cried Carl, the little white cucumber.

"Stop choking me!!" yelled Tammy, the big red tomato.

Benny was in one gigantic mess and found himself so twisted and confused, he didn't know how to even begin to straighten out the mess he had made of his vines. He had been so selfish and had only thought about himself. Iris helped him to remember that it wasn't just about doing the things he wanted to do. It was about something much bigger.

As he looked around, Benny became very sad at the mess he had caused and all the problems he had created for his friends because of his poor choices. But he also reassured himself that he could never mess up too much that the gardener wouldn't be able to straighten it out.

That is just what happened!

As the mud puddles began to dry up, the gardener was able to return. And sure enough, all the twisted mess was unwound and Benny soon found himself once again bound to the tiny strings and two stakes. How happy he was to feel the presence and warmth of THE SUN and to see the beautiful blue sky.

The little vegetable garden produced a bountiful harvest all summer long. Benny learned to respect the peas and never again trespassed on the cucumbers. He considered his travel each day and tried to stay on the right path. He didn't get carried away and choke out the tomatoes ever again.

They needed room to grow just like he did. He remembered that those little white cucumbers were also special seeds that had been saved, just like he was. As long as he focused on THE SUN and grew up, there was plenty of room to run and he would continue to grow and grow and grow.

There was bushel after bushel of green beans, plenty of peas for neighbors and friends, cucumbers for canning pickles, and tomatoes to last for months and months.

Benny felt the joy of being a unique seed that had been saved again that summer. He understood that he was a special seed because God had created him to be special and nothing he could do would ever change that! They were all special seeds in the garden and they were all "saved" to produce special fruit. This was the determined will and plan of the Master Bean-Maker. Benny also knew that he had some free will choices to make each year on his own. Because of his experiences that year in the garden, he now understood the importance of making good choices.

The gardener desired a certain pathway for him and tried to show him the best direction to take; however, the final choice was always up to Benny.

Unlike before, now he realized that he should not concentrate on his own selfish desires. Instead, he should follow the pathway to THE SUN, as best he could. This way offered peace, joy, and produced an abundant crop.

Even when he did not make good choices, the gardener would still straighten out the mess and guide him back toward the son.

"For by grace you have been saved through faith. And this is not your own doing, it is the gift of God, not a result of works, so that no one may boast." (Ephesians 2:8-9)

23

Kathy Bingham Powell is both humbled and excited to present the publication of her second book about her original garden friends, Benny the bean seed and Iris the bulb, and to introduce some of their other garden pals She has carefully combined her two great loves of gardening, and reading picture books to continue her mother's original ministry of "saving the seeds". She firmly believes that both children and adults can be ministered to through lessons from the garden and carefully chosen picture books. She is inspired by scripture, particularly the Parable of the Sower and believes that seeds can be planted in her literary garden as well as her vegetable and flower garden. The seeds of her own personal faith are preserved through both her private collection of picture books and through her replanting of "saved seeds" from last year's vegetable garden. She lives a simple life as a preschool teacher, loving wife of over thirty years and the mother of three grown children. She devotes her winter to being in the classroom with two, three, and four year olds and spending time in her literary "Tiny Seeds Garden" at home. She donates a large part of her summertime to helping young children grow and share vegetables and flowers from their very own Kinder Garden – a part of the church community garden. Planting "saved" seeds from the garden and reading and sharing from this personal collection of picture books is her way of preserving her own childhood faith and spreading God's love into the world.

Printed in the United States
by Baker & Taylor Publisher Services